Cold Cuts on Wry

ABBY KENIGSBERG

Cold Cuts on Wry

© 2022 Abby Kenigsberg

ISBN 978-1-66787-038-0

eBook ISBN 978-1-66787-039-7

Dedicated to

Matthew, Ezra, and Amos

Lisa, Amy, and Emily

Raina, Joshua, Zachary,

Emerson, Magnolia, Lila, and Aster

To the Reader:

I hate ironing but love irony. Ironing's lonely – it's just you, the cloth, and the iron.

But with irony, you aren't alone. Someone is sharing with you what's under the surface.

When people laugh, a bond is formed. Sharing what frightens you, what you wonder about, or what amuses you builds community.

My hope is that my poetry makes you smile, and that smile sheds a small light on any weakness or worries you might have.

A friend once told me that as his mother lay dying, she suddenly brightened up, called his name, and said to him, "Remember, with laughter."

A smile = First base

A chuckle = Second base

A guffaw = Third base

Enjoy!

Contents

Humor

Change Your Attitude

Change your attitude, Mother used to bark
I never listened
And just the other day I picked up some crazy
Doctor talk

There's a chemical out there named Sarah Tonin
I don't know if they named it after the girl
Who invented it or she was somebody's girlfriend
Anyway Sarah Tonin can make you happier

They say it swishes around in your brain
Long enough to change your attitude

Frankly, the whole thing is pretty weird
How a chemical named Sarah Tonin
Can get messages to your brain to make you happier
I don't know
Maybe some rat in a lab looked goofy
Because he overdosed on Sarah Tonin
Maybe that's how it started

I myself like a drink called Margarita
I know, Margarita's alcohol
And the same doctors pushing Sarah Tonin
Say, *Don't get involved with alcohol*

But alcohol goes a long way

If your phone's dead

Or your TV won't work

Grab Sarah Tonin or Margarita

Either girl can change your attitude

The Big Squeeze

When the Gnat and the Boa sit down for tea

There's always a rumble from a meddlesome Bee:

"Don't go there, fella, 'cause he uses ghee

To swallow you down when you think you're home free."

The Gnat said, "I talked to the mighty constrictor.

When we sit down for tea, no one's the victor.

The Boa has told me I'm just small potatoes—

He doesn't like me or sun-dried tomatoes."

"That's what you think," boomed the Shark from the deep.

"Wait till he wants a long winter's sleep.

He'll grab you and toss you right down his gullet.

I've seen him grab onions and a mountain of mullet."

Boa admitted at times he might slip

Perhaps at McDonald's where he could get a good grip

On children who are downing those greasy French fries,

Big Macs and soda that reach up to their eyes.

At tea he also deflected the rumors

That he squeezed runners and cute baby boomers.

But he admitted to squeezing at rich Goldman Sachs

'Cause he couldn't resist girls in blazers and slacks.

By now the Gnat was beginning to doubt

That he'd always be safe near the Boa's big snout

So he packed up his tea set and made the decision

To get Boa a job in nuclear fission.

Civilization

As my dog waits to be washed and trimmed

At the Luv-My-Pet Salon

He wears a resolute expression

Like fathers attending a season of

Middle-school violin concerts.

Dogs exchange a similar glance as they

Pass each other on the way to the lock-up

To await the Luv-My-Pet Salon experience.

Oh, to run through the meadows

To pursue gamey squirrels

And make friends by scent

Instead of succumbing to

Hibiscus baths and undignified air-blowing

That itches my skin

And the erotic spray smelling

Like a fruit salad.

I survive the Luv-My-Pet Salon experience

By thinking of it as

Prelude to a serious nap

Where I can dream of running in the fields

And discover new friends by the scent of their turds

Paying no attention to household rules

And the deficiencies of civilization.

Icarus

Sitting at a window

I watch the house next door

Sunny concrete walls and a brown-shingled roof

Where birds swing by

They look effortless

As they swoop and change direction

They tip one wing down

Banking banking

Somehow they know

If they tip one wing

They'll go

Banking banking

If I were a bird could I do that?

Doubtful

When I skied

I questioned the principle that

Shifting my weight while up in the air

Could change my direction

Yet birds dip one wing and there they go

Banking banking

Who told them how to do that?

Do birds have flying lessons?

Do birds pay attention?

Children don't.

One day Daedalus is supposed to have muttered

Some kids never learn.

Warning To Women Who Buy Fancy Red Cars

Hey, you old ladies out looking for thrills

Or girls who are rich and laugh at the bills

Or cuties too lazy to check out an auto

Or snobs who like showrooms and call red, tomato

Or consumers impressed with remarkable traction

Or lascivious women looking for action

Or those of you bored with the old family car

Tesla lies in wait by raising the bar

So if you're dreaming of a rose-colored chariot

Beware the car maker: he may prove an Iscariot

Those Were The Days

Baby alligator stretched in the sun

On his mama's back

Oh yes, he thought, *this is lovely*

And the mama smiled and understood

Oh yes, joy rides on my back

Oh yes, opined the Fox

Always on the prowl for a crunchy snack

Baby on his mama's back

Would be a dainty morsel

But the mama saw

The willow tree sway

As the Fox moved behind it

Oh yes, we'll get out of the sun

Right now, she figured,

To keep the baby safe

And his skin enchanting

Later they came to a bend in the river

There sat the Cougar sunning on his rock

Oh yes, he mused, *that's the sight*

Of a lovely two-course dinner

But the mama spotted grasses

Waving as the Cougar

Crouched on his rock

Oh yes, I'll slip away from here

To keep the little one unharmed

The baby, now grown, savors

Memories he has of his mother

Just lazing all day in the sunshine, mama and me

Frank, You Old Goat

If you ever find yourself a student at a cockamamie summer poetry program, you may fall heir to the irksome assignment of writing a Petrarchan sonnet.

Never mind that you live in the twenty-first century. Your focus must now be on an irreverent time in fourteenth-century Italy.

I say "irreverent" because Francesco Petrarch, who perfected the sonnet in question, turns out to have been quite the swinger. For a guy born in 1304 he did OK. Although his career was in the Church and he wasn't allowed to marry, he fathered two adorable bambini, Giovanni and Francesca. But the babies were hardly his only pastime.

Frank found another way to amuse himself and drive students crazy for centuries.

If you must create a Petrarchan sonnet, don't pray or cogitate. Make a template. You need space for fourteen numbered lines. On the right, note the rhyme required. Breathe deeply. Proceed. Concoct eight lines.

You're not home free. Frank throws you a curve, but forewarned is forearmed.

In deciding on the six remaining lines, you must grab a different rhyme scheme. You'll never throw the fourteen lines together like a fine Italian salad, where radicchio, arugula, and dandelion greens become indistinguishable.

The fact that Francesco Petrarch lived to be seventy years old avoiding plagues means that he must have done something right. It may have been imbibing fine wines or siring bambini or writing Petrarchan sonnets. Practice any or all of these and you'll probably be all right.

Goings On By The Nile

cleo was sexy and swivel-hipped

pharaohs liked incest and eucalypt

but this is all we know for sure

you hadda watch for a saboteur—

that could be why in ancient days

egyptians only moved sideways

On Seeing An Apple Ad In The NY Times

Ya got me Apple—by the sackful

I own an iPad, Phone, and Air

It's all gorgeous, sleek and app-full

Designed with utmost savoir faire

But when I saw an ad for dreamers

A hero gold in sweaty glow

Then I knew I should examine

Crafty Apple's undertow

Like Riefenstahl's dreams of glory

Apple sells a bedtime story

So when you buy its fine technology

Caveat emptor: iMythology

Family Life

This Time

This time he started it
By saying I criticized him all the time.
I added that the rest of the time
I was taking care of him.
"Don't take care of me," he bellows
So I let him walk home in the rain.

This time I try to make amends
By proposing we go to his favorite museum.
"What a great idea," he smiles
More cheerful than necessary.

This time I shop for his favorite foods
And this time he puts them away.

This time when I come home from work
He says, as we often do,
"It doesn't get better than this."
Standing close to him I say,
"Oh yes it does—
You said I criticized you all the time."
And he says,
"Well, it doesn't seem like criticism to you."

And I figured since he was explaining to me
Why it could be interpreted
That when I was criticizing him
Maybe I wasn't,
Maybe we were OK … this time.

Rascal Fire

Fire came to my house as a master of disguise

With a rascal's *danse*

And an inscrutable nature

He scorched and shattered the walls

But he cavorted on the dining room table

Leaving it singed and blistered

While ignoring

The Book of Psalms that lay

Upon it

I'm guessing he danced a victory lap into the kitchen

And chortled as he left

The refrigerator door

An oozing stretch of silly putty

I imagine he shimmied past the jewels

Secreted in a metal cabinet

And left unscathed my ivory netsukes

Hidden deep in an oatmeal of cold black ash

Whirling into the closet he

Clearly ran roughshod over nylon and acrylic

I am nature at its mightiest, which you are not

He snickered as he destroyed the garments while

Bypassing nature's fibers of silk and linen

Leaving them smiling and amenable

To a new beginning

I wouldn't be surprised if

The mischievous demon

Signaled the neighbors

When he was finally exhausted

To give them time

To steal the silver

And when I asked the dry cleaner to restore my

My raccoon coat of rowdy days

My husband understood better than I

Fire's impenetrable signature

Your coat glistens as before, my dear, but

It will always smell like a good wood fire.

Princess Dreams

A tiny girl of three

Wails

As she's belted into her car seat

Seeing only the black plastic headrest

Inches from her nose

She's handed a tiny gossamer bag

With a satin drawstring

And a chunk of a sparkling garnet inside

Silent as she

Opens and closes the bag

Bewitched by the smooth silken strands

That remind her

Of her dreams

Whiteness

In the nursery school pageant

Her plans were to become a

Bavarian Crème

Donut

But once she wound white crepe-paper

Streamers around her

Neck and

White satin

Around her

Torso

And masterminded a crown of

Scotch-taped marshmallows to sit

On her brow

She became

A calcimine snow princess or

Maybe even the Duchess of

Alba

And at the conclusion of said pageant

Her parents with wallet,

White bichon

White cowboy boots

Awarded their princess

White primroses

And two squirts of

Whipped cream

Balanced briefly

Atop a frothy vanilla

Shake

Little Lone Ranger

Boy of seven

Buckles plastic helmet

Fierce as the blowing wind

Throws one leg over the bike seat

Looking ready for a gale force

He pushes on

Then he stops

Brings his purple-sneakered feet back to earth

Hangs his helmet on the handlebar with

Nonchalance

Then like all masters of the trail

Strides cockily on

Responsible for his own travels

To breakfast at the Inn

With Mom and Dad

News From The Interior

Chanting emanates from the interior

Victorious sounds pierce the stillness

Strange repetition

Pervades and distends the atmosphere

Chants undulate and continue

A crescendo builds

An elder follows the sensuous calls

Through steam and unremitting heat

Finally the warrior appears

"How was the shower, dear?"

"It was just a shower," the seventeen-year-old replies.

Trickle-Down Theory

Trickle-down theory

Works for

Water

Doesn't work for

Money

If you made it

You don't like to trickle it

Generational trickle?

Doesn't work either

A seventy-year-old's sense of time

Doesn't trickle down to a forty-year-old who's

In a hurry

A fourteen-year-old and his dad?

No trickle there either

Circle theory?

Maybe

Goes around

Maybe

Comes around

Household Maneuvers

I was never much of a housekeeper

But when they told me

I was dizzy because

Some odd calcium chips

Had fallen out of my inner ear

And were lying, hatter-scatter, in my

Vestibule

I thought it was time to

Pay attention

The doc just

Twisted my head

As if it were a cork

On a good rosé

I thought

Amazing

He cleaned up the rubbish

By twisting my head

That Epley maneuver

May be good housekeeping for the ear

But when I can clean my kitchen

With just a twist of my head

That'll be the day …

Maybe Solomon Didn't Always Get It Right

"If you were me,

What would you choose—the kids' visit or a haircut?"

I asked my husband,

The family Solomon in charge of wise judgments.

I, sturdy as a jellyfish,

Was seeking advice.

He, packed with Biblical assurance,

Swiveled away from his computer and

Faced me with a confident smile.

"Easy!" he boomed. "Give up the haircut."

I didn't want to hear that.

"What?" I exploded. "Give up the haircut? Are you crazy?"

Now pumped up against his certitude

Was my own.

Risking all on untested shears,

I scooted from the room,

Cancelled one haircutter,

Booked another who had time that worked.

The next day, happily shorn and waiting for the kids,

I smiled at my dear husband.

Even the guy in the Bible

Didn't always get it right.

Haibun

Haiku

Summer night beach fire

Wood crackles in the stillness

Children meditate

Narrative

On the morning of the bonfire children and parents discuss
the weather as seriously as sailors looking to the horizon
for a coming storm. In the afternoon the children bolt up
and down the beach hunting wood—a signal contest
of endurance and power.

Bigger kids retrieve water-logged pieces of broken piers.
Little ones present hollow sticks with flags of dried seaweed.
Parents, in the same game, hoist logs to create seating. Someone
presents a rusted metal cage for kindling and a wrecked chair of
mysterious origin.

The beach house is ransacked for newspapers, chocolate bars,
boxes of graham crackers, sacrificial marshmallows.

Silence descends.

Matches keep failing. Finally a fire. The rumpled children shout admiration
for shooting flames and explosions from a damp but burning log. They show
off their prized golden marshmallows and drop crackers in the sand.
An even deeper silence. Kids' eyes get larger. Their bodies relax.

Before they sink into sleep they agree,
That was the best bonfire ever.

Boxes For Moving To Texas

Seven AM

The grocery store is empty and cold

No buzz of commerce yet

I go past the glass tank

One lobster crawls over still ones

Disturbing a greenish gray ooze

Fat white chicken breasts

Rotate on a spit in an oven called "Inferno"

Can I have some boxes?

I'm at Customer Service

We ain't got 'em now, lady, too early

They told me to come early

Who said that?

I didn't get his name

I smile to show I can take it

Come back later

He turns away

I consider produce

Zealous stalks of rhubarb

Frame verdant puffs of broccoli

You got some boxes?

He goes behind the dark swinging doors

At the back of the store

I wait and wait

He appears from another direction with boxes

Great. Thank you, I need them

The sweet scent of just-baked bagels

Propels me to the deli

You got low-fat cheese?

Yeah, what d'ya want

What's you got?

Swiss, muenster, or alpine. What d'ya want?

One pound muenster, sliced thin please

Can't make muenster thin, lady, it's too soft

I walk by the lobsters again,

Curious to see if the live one is still moving

While I wait to pay, I read that "Gone with the Wind" is 75

And George Clooney got married

Outside, a damp New York wind pushes

Me and the boxes

Backward

I bend down and press on

It's a long way to Texas

Alone

Their trip is long but
Together they
Motor through the Pine Barrens' darkness
And by rows of placid cornstalks

Finally they trudge up the stairs
To their cabin by the sea
The lights don't work
Moonlight does

Dragging satchels and groceries
She heads to the kitchen
Kills ants on the counter, empties dishwasher
Refrigerates milk, yogurt, chicken, and cheese
Cautiously pinches the peaches and plums

He meanders to his deck chair to commune with
Venus and whatever else is out there

She brings his Glenlivet
Ice cubes
Clink in the stillness

                       He asks her
                       If she sees Venus
She's never sure

                       He tells her

If it's big and bright it's
probably Venus.

North Star is almost true north

But not as bright as, say, the Big Dipper.

Big Dipper? Where?

She doesn't see it.

Damn.

It's damp. And no-see-ums interrupt the night.

She goes in

And goes to bed

Wondering,

What's he thinking about out there?

Marcus Aurelius? Dinner?

She remembers

Him motionless

Studying a tree bending in the wind

Or enraptured by the rotating crystals

In his rainbow-maker

Because the sunbeams are more than 90 million miles away.

Guy's an odd duck

She goes to sleep

Glad

She changed the sheets.

Hospital

space in a dim closet contains

a stretcher with plastic sheets

a hardened pillow

a patient and

an expert

documenting the old man's muscle

as it inexorably shoots blood through

a network of tired arteries

the patient sleeps to avoid data

the technician works hard to gather more

and I look from my husband

to inscrutable images on the monitor

in this narrow place

I could easily touch either man

but am

alone

Flowers Dying

I thought of you when I stopped

To look at those tulips

Dominating the kitchen table

Silently fading and falling apart

They are more dear than ever

Their delicate pink

Becomes deep purple as if in agony

And they droop in a farewell bow

I couldn't stop looking

The more I looked

The more real they became

Hyperreal, you might say

The transient tulips caught me

Arrested me

Arrested time

The World Around Us

Sedaris

The Book People crowd, happily awaiting

The writer's wry observations,

Trade stories about his eminent wit.

Cute legs, I think as he appears in a kilt.

He enchants us with new tales about his screwball family

And concludes by recounting the critic

Who barked, "Well roared, Lion!"

At an earlier gig.

He smiles as he scans

One hundred fans

Cushioning one hundred books to their breasts

Lined up dutifully for their names to be

Inscribed in his latest opus.

Since I have number ninety-eight, I plan to leave.

As the crowd pushes me past the smiling writer

With cute legs

I tell him, "Well roared, Lion" ...

That's from *A Midsummer Night's Dream* ...

Shakespeare."

He stops and considers.

"I didn't know that," he says,

Grateful for new information

Floating above

A plethora of the usual adulation.

He glances at the book cushioned in my elbow

And at the crowd in line.

He scrutinizes me again

And keeps ninety-eight fans waiting as

He motions me forward and writes

Well roared, Lion!

In my book.

The Down Escalator
At Bloomingdale's

Something weightless floats past me on the escalator—

A cloud?

Couldn't be

It's a long white puffy plastic dress bag

Tethered to a lithe young Asian woman

She glides down

As the escalator descends, wearing

Thin white flip-flops

Tight black pants and a wisp of a white silk blouse

That spills low on her shoulder

She skims to the bottom like a soft wind and

Floats rapidly out the door

I march along, curious to see what vehicle

A blade of grass would drive

She's left no trace when I get there

A shiny white Bentley whisks away

Anticipation

Luminous sky at dawn

Charged with hints of possibilities and

A rich day to come

Like the theatre

Before a performance

The exquisite air of expectation

As audience and actor

Silently agree to a fantastical game

Of make-believe.

Soon.

Not yet.

Tree Secrets

An uncommon maple
Burst forth in red this autumn
While others
Girded themselves in green

This maple rejoiced
In flashy crimson
Rollicking each day
Until the blaze
Diminished

Then she joined
The rest in predictable burnished browns of autumn

What did the baritone of an oak
Or the tenor elm signal at night to this wanton?

What was she celebrating before
She disguised herself
Finally
In the dutiful, sallow colors of late fall?

True Grit

They cut down

The mighty oak

On my neighbor's lawn today

Slices lying on the grass

Expose rings

Spilling into each other

Reminders of

Trembling limbs and bending boughs

The majestic tree's

Scabs betray

Battles with

Winds and

Squalls

Now dazzling witnesses to

Perseverance

Florida Fishing Pier

Fishermen are here all right

Anxious to catch a fish or two

Old men with thinning beards and

Seasoned faces

Younger ones with

Triple-decker toolboxes

Knives and hooks all in place

Balls of tightly coiled plastic lines

And newfangled rods

Each rests a foot on the rail

And reads the shadows

In the sea

Or glances sideways

At a neighbor's bucket

Where the already doomed

Swirl about

They stand alone or in small groups

While young hawkers

In woolen Bob Marley hats

And ripped jeans work the pier talking up

Better bait

Smarter hooks

Teenagers gather to watch

Sturdy pelicans

Dive-bombing for dinner

Or spot the rare shark

Slicing through the water

Moms are there too

Watching toddlers

Run up and down the pier

Past hooks and gulls

And invisible fishing line

Once in a while a woman rubs

Her husband's neck

As he stands motionless

Like the player waiting in left field

To catch something

And have a story

For later

Over a beer

On Being Bitten By A Solenopsis Invicta

I'm disappointed by your aggressive response

To a purely innocent gesture of moving one stone.

I didn't know you had a grand design

Or that you were into major architecture

Or that you had workers digging tunnels

Flattening highways

Carving embankments and

Bivouacs.

I never knew an advance party was already securing food!

Your attack could have been avoided

If you knew who you were dealing with.

In the long run

I'll (maybe) outlast you

So don't bite me again with your fancy formic acid.

Or how about this idea?

You go your way

And I'll go mine.

First Thing We Do: Kill All The Lawyers

Aristotle says

The law is leaden

It cannot see

The workings of the soul

Today we have

The Supremes

Suave assassins or devastating advocates

Who do it all without

Compromising their gentility

Good news, Aristotle

Mix one part lead

With nine parts politics

Fold in the thrill of

Ascendency and

You got it: Justice.

Flan From Afar

Early Sunday morning the farmers market

Sprouts again

Workers unfurl

Chrome yellow and red

Striped signs

Creating the hubbub of

A small Italian town square

Hawking

Everything from fire cider to

Keto bread

Soon the Texas sun stifles

Shopping fervor

Leaving

Three- and four-year-olds

To accelerate runs

Through the pulsating water fountains

I find a shaded bench

To sit and relish my

Chilled espresso flan

Soon I notice another is

Copying my every move

He turns his body

To watch me eat

He opens and closes his mouth

When I do

He follows the spoon as

It goes from cup to lip

We are in a duet

Now his father

Carries him away

Papoose-like

I smile and wave

As he fixes on my face

He's six months old and

Has far to go

Before he tastes

The pungent tang of

Espresso flan

The Milk Bucket

Fashionable jeans today

Are ripped and rubbed.

They cost more if they look worn out.

The maker tells you,

In a note affixed with ratty twine,

How lucky you are to

Pay more

For crap.

Explaining the charm of wrecked things isn't easy.

My mother-in-law,

Her life spent

Scrubbing, saving, and shining,

Was mystified by my antique milk bucket,

A wooden relic with chipped soft-blue paint.

"Explain to me why you bought that,"

She asked brightly

Thinking she'd finally understand.

How do you explain to someone who works for

A brighter tomorrow

About the charm of a pale yesterday?

Or why you overpaid for a splintered

Little milk bucket?

I cannot

But the guy who markets

Those wrecked Wranglers

Understands

Fashion is for those with

Too much money and

Too little spine.

Le Madras Rouge

(After a Painting by Henri Matisse)

Matisse's woman

In a bright blue gown

And a clincher of a red hat

Looks at us

Engaged.

A master of placement and position

She sits

Arms propped on a chair

(*Do you like my hat?*)

Head twisted ever so coyly

Hat angled ever so boldly

She gazes at us from below

Knowing she looks good.

She waits for a tiny cup

Of espresso

She will caress daintily

As she shows

The bright blue gown and the red hat

She decided to wear

At the last minute

Because she knew

It would attract

The guy with the easel.

Religion

Just A Challah

Who knew two gigantic bowls

Have to be there

Who knew there was a

Separation

Even before there was a

Marriage

Who knew the wet stuff

Has its own playground

And the dry stuff

Over there

Nobody told me you needed

Eight cups of flour

I'm making one sweet loaf

That would remind me

Of Grandma Mary

Not the wall

At the Mexican border.

So, wait a minute —

The yeast (wet bowl) is already rising

While I combine dry stuff

In the other giant bowl?

Now the beaten eggs

Invade the moist guys?

I'm beginning to feel like I'm between

The Montagues and the Capulets.

Over here I keep adding flour

Until it looks like

One big homunculus.

Confusion. I need to knead?

Now that the two bowls are united

We have a second uprising.

Now that the two sides have united

I wait. It rises

And I punch it down

And knead again.

More long division

Braid time —

No wonder my no-nonsense Grandma Ida

Just filled two loaf pans

And thrust them into the oven

(No one told me to pre-heat)

Not as tragic

As the young lovers.

My kitchen produced two

Three-dimensional

Edible

Digestible

Loaves.

Jewish Women Baking

"Hurray up, make some bread," Abraham,

The oldest Hebrew,

Was supposed to have said to Sarah,

The oldest Hebrew wife.

"Company's coming!"

That was a while ago—

God only knows when.

A thousand years later

Jewish men were still yelling,

"Hurray up!"

To their wives

Waiting for the dough to rise

But men knew there wasn't time—

They were heading for the Promised Land.

Four thousand years later

Snappy Jewish women,

Well versed in the #metoo movement

Not waiting for their husbands to call the shots

Reading cookbooks called

Millennial Kosher

And *Twenty Ways to Stuff a Challah*

Braiding dough

Peppered with garlic,

Spices and dates,

Stuffed with goat cheese

And figs,

Reflect the rich lives

Of the challah-makers

And while the bread is rising

And life continues,

Jewish women wonder,

Will we be on the run again?

The Horns Of A Dilemma

I see the muddy hooves

Of a ram

When I hear the primitive sound of the shofar

Summoning my ancient tribe

I am moved by the sound

Commanding me now to stop

Be still

Listen

Yet I am buoyed by the silver horns

Of Handel's Messiah

Shimmering with grace

Delicacy

And the beauty of passion

Thoughts Ex Cathedra

I say, "Thanks for the sugar" to the friendly German grocer

Whom I admire for her robust smile,

Confident hand and boisterous laugh.

Her eyes narrow and she says,

"I have a Jewish friend and

Her grandmother never measured anything."

I wonder

When she says "Jewish" is there hatred

Deep down

I hide the thought as I

Wear a false and fearless smile

And walk into the sunlight.

No Point Holding A Grudge

Galilei and Barberini were college buddies.

Later their directions diverged.

Galilei wrapped himself

In an unholy love of the skies.

Tell me your secrets,

He would whisper to the moon.

Beautiful Luna,

Just call me Galileo.

Barberini went into a political subspecialty—

Religion, they called it.

He loved it so much

He became Urban the Pope

And then he declared

The earth is the center of the universe

And I the center of policy.

Meanwhile, one swoony night

A light bulb—though not yet invented—

Switched on in Galileo's head:

It's the earth taking center-stage ...

Running circles around the sun.

He wrote a book on his discoveries

Putting the Church's ideas

Into the mouth of a simpleton called

Simplicio.

Urban was not amused:

You keep searching for new ideas up there

And I'll have you tortured or burned to death down here.

Kneel before me, ordered Urban, the tips

Of his red silk slippers pointing directly

At Galileo. *And say you're only guessing.*

Galileo did as he was told.

Still, Urban never forgave him.

Three centuries later

Pope John Paul suggested

The Church reconsider.

Thirteen years the Church pondered

Then pronounced Galileo right …

No point holding a grudge.

Dear To Someone

there is a tiny grey baby squirrel lying in the road

dead

I avoid him

my dog, on the other hand,

has a whetted appetite

grey squirrel au poivre, he thinks as

we move on

the baby's soft silvery coat must have been dear

to someone other than my dog

maybe his mother

we move on

I am reminded of the rats that became pets

for children hiding from Nazis

in ghetto sewers

much to the consternation of their parents

we move on

the next day the soft grey body has been flattened

by a tire

and on the next day

it is gone

we move on

You Are What You Eat

Regard the old adage:

You are what you eat

Reflect on what's faddish

With signature treats

The Aztecs glowed

With mountains of chia

While chopped liver was king

For the guys from Judea

Egypt Then

What happened to Jews in the Land of the Sphinx?

Did someone slip Pharaoh the wrong kind of drinks?

Or give bad advice at Heliopolis Links?

Or maybe they promised to smooth out the kinks

On the rumor that Cleo could use a few shrinks.

Did they make pyramids with embarrassing chinks?

Or paint eyes with kohl so that nobody blinks?

Whatever they did, they harnessed a jinx

By crossing the sea in just forty winks.

Two Dreams, A Nightmare, And A Vision

Superhero Dream

I fall asleep reading my kid's superhero comic

I dream that while my husband dozes on the couch

A burglar appears

I steer him to the fake jewelry in the bedroom

Then I call the cops

A lady cop arrives

She wants a quick shower

While husband sleeps

Burglar burgles,

Cop showers

I get pissed off when I hear her using my hair dryer

Burglar appears with a hacksaw

Now he goes for my husband's neck

I bellow like a savage

Lift the miscreant high in the air

Carry him to the balcony

Where I hurl

Over the railing

First the burglar

TAKE THAT

And then the hacksaw

AND THAT

I look over the side and see

The burglar and the hacksaw

In a flattened heap on the ground

I strut inside

All in a day's work

Giraffe Talk

I dreamed I went on a fact-finding mission in Africa.

I wanted to interview the tallest animal in the world.

I found a millennial giraffe wearing a snappy camo design

Who had his head up a 12-foot acacia.

Having spied me, he stuck his neck out.

I told him I was sorry to disturb his meal.

No problem, he replied.

I got right down to business.

There's something I need to ask you, I said.

He evaluated me as he chewed,

His pouchy lips swaying from side to side.

Shoot, he muttered between chomps.

How do you survive, I asked, *with such a weird connection*

Between your head and the rest of you?

It must be tough with a little brain and an unusual neck.

I don't look at it that way, he said.

First, lots of animals are strange.

I think humans are really strange.

You have such complicated brains and nervous systems

That you can't figure out how to love yourself,

Let alone your fellow man.

We giraffes, we just worry about eating, sleeping, and mating.

We look out for each other.

You guys are always complaining about your existence.

What do you mean? I asked.

Take Hamlet, said the giraffe. *He talks about heart-ache,*
And the whips and scorns of time.

Now I was really puzzled.
Hamlet? What do you know about Hamlet?

The giraffe chuckled.
Long necks get you places, he said.
Hamlet's brain didn't help him. He was one messed-up dude.
My long neck has never bothered me.
We get along out here in the savannah.
There's no animal I complain about.

He went back to the acacia.
I waited to see if he had more to say.
His frowzy lips selected only baby greens.
Then he turned toward me from across the branches.

But there are some bad ones.
I have to watch out for lions and crocodiles.
Lions are real phonies.
They got a big roar but make the women do all the work.

And have you noticed the yap on a crocodile?
Slime. Just slime.

At that moment I woke up ... with a stiff neck.

Cowgirl Nightmare

One day I discovered I had shoe prints on my face. There was the print of a sneaker on my left side and the print of an army boot on my right side. I wasn't sure it was an army boot. But I did notice that the indentations were much deeper than the print of the sneaker.

I wasn't too worried about them and went to my haircutter for the usual trim. He turned me to face the mirror when he finished. Bending low to my left ear, he whispered "You know, Abby, you should really get those shoe marks off your face."

"Oh, OK. But I don't know how."

"Could I remove them for you?"

"Sure."

He rubbed my cheeks with some very strong stuff. It smelled like nail polish remover. It didn't remove the marks.

"Never mind," I said. "I'm going to find out who put those marks on me."

Now I was in my college dorm. I was in a long, dark hallway. Nobody seemed to be around, and I decided to open every door on my way down the hall.

I opened the first door. "Anybody here?"
The floor was newly washed and smelled of bleach. The bright yellow walls smelled of fresh paint. "Anybody here?"

No one answered.

I opened the second door, and the room also had a newly washed floor and fresh paint. "Anybody here?"

No one was in that room either.

I went to the third door (you know, there's always three in dreams), opened it, and yelled, "Anybody here?"

Nobody there, the same floor. But these walls were covered in silver paper.

Then I saw a group of college girls—three of them—hanging around in the hallway. They were much younger and slimmer than I. They all had long blonde hair and were wearing tight blue jeans, cowboy shirts, and boots.

"Who put these marks on my face?" I yelled, approaching them.

The girls abruptly stopped talking and turned as a group to face me.

Two girls swore, "I didn't put marks on your face." But the third girl said, "I did because you stole my orchid." I did see an orchid in my mind's eye, but I knew I didn't steal her orchid.

"I didn't steal your orchid," I told her, "and I think it's pretty lousy of you to mark my face because of something you *thought* I did. I'm going to report you to Carissa because she's in charge."

I went to her office to report the cowgirl and the footprints. Carissa wasn't there but her assistant, who looked like she might have had shoe prints on *her* face, said the boss had left.

Then I woke up and checked the mirror. The shoe prints were gone.

Activity In A French Toile Bedroom

I am shown to my bedroom in a Greek resort town

To discover

French toile covering the walls,

The bed, the bedstead, the bureau,

The closet, the lampshades and pillows

This fabric illustrates the pastoral world of Marie Antoinette

There's no dirt, no dust

Just vignettes of country living in never-never land

I am fascinated by a couple picnicking:

She's in a sweeping taffeta skirt and romantic bosomy bodice

He's in silk stockings and shoes with fancy buckles

Some scenes peek out between graceful branches:

Bunnies gambol with sweet canines on a hunt

While a young man carries his musket cheerfully

As if in a ballet

There's a young woman balancing

A charming basket of laundry on her head

Down two rows a youth plays his flute

It's a pastoral activities spreadsheet of the 1700's.

Now I study the rest of the room:

Above the bed

A large painting of a muscular man

Seated at a grand piano,

Dramatically bent over the keyboard

Wearing a twenty-first-century bright yellow linen jacket

His hands bear down on the keys

As he plays the final, assertive chords of a concerto.

I leave to join my group for a mighty Greek repast of

Lamb, figs, octopus, moussaka,

Souvlaki, baklava, grapes, apricots, and ouzo.

When I return, the toile is still jumping

The bodice on the picnicker is rumpled

A satyr is playing the flute, and the bunnies,

More of them, are still hopping.

As for the pianist, I hear the final chords of Rachmaninoff.

The guy's good.

Addendum

Gertie Stein

let's drink a toast to gertie stein

whose verbs would dance but not decline

who saw herself as avant garde

and hoisted rules on her petard

rude stein

gerr rude

gerr stein

popinjay

pop in play

pop and stay

wrap it up

rap it up

rap the cup

wrap up the pup

silver bells

sylvan bells

silver knells

silver belles

hell's bells

My thanks to the following:

Susan Luton, gifted editor

Katherine Moore, extraordinary wordsmith

My sister, Deborah Cohen

My friends, Catia Chapin and Amanda Pope